D1068640

12 MAMMALS
BACK FROM THE BRINK

by Nancy Furstinger

12 STORY LIBRARY

www.12StoryLibrary.com

Copyright © 2015 by Peterson Publishing Company, North Mankato, MN 56003. All rights reserved. No part of this book may be reproduced or utilized in any form or by any means without written permission from the publisher.

12-Story Library is an imprint of Peterson Publishing Company and Press Room Editions.

Produced for 12-Story Library by Red Line Editorial

Photographs ©: Curioso/Shutterstock Images, cover, 1; Silver-john/Shutterstock Images, 4; Thorsen Nieder/Shutterstock Images, 6; davemhuntphotography/Shutterstock Images, 7, 27; USFWS/AP Images, 8; Jo Crebbin/Shutterstock Images, 10, 11; Holly Kuchera/Shutterstock Images, 12; Weddell Images/Shutterstock Images, 13; Jean-Edouard Rozey/Shutterstock Images, 14; Mighty Sequoia Studio/Shutterstock Images, 15; Dominic Laniewicz/Shutterstock Images, 17, 29 (top); Beth Swanson/Shutterstock Images, 18; Bildagentur Zoonar GmbH/Shutterstock Images, 19; David Osborn/Shutterstock Images, 20; Kathryn Willmott/Shutterstock Images, 22; Xiebiyun/Shutterstock Images, 23, 29 (bottom); Tom Reichner/Shutterstock Images, 24; Wild Art/Shutterstock Images, 25; Volodymyr Burdiak/Shutterstock Images, 26

ISBN
978-1-63235-003-9 (hardcover)
978-1-63235-063-3 (paperback)
978-1-62143-044-5 (hosted ebook)

Library of Congress Control Number: 2014937244

Printed in the United States of America
Mankato, MN
June, 2014

Go beyond the book. Get free, up-to-date content on this topic at 12StoryLibrary.com.

TABLE OF CONTENTS

GIANT PANDAS RELEASED INTO BAMBOO FORESTS

Giant pandas don't start out giant. They weigh the same as a stick of butter at birth. Panda cubs' fur is snowy white. After several weeks, they start growing patches of black fur. Adult giant pandas spend 12 hours a day eating. On the menu is bamboo.

They use their powerful jaws and sharp teeth to crush the shoots and leaves. But when bamboo trees became harder to find, so did the pandas.

Giant pandas used to live all across southern and eastern

Pandas are great climbers. Sometimes they even sleep in trees.

IUCN RED LIST

The International Union for the Conservation of Nature (IUCN) keeps a list of all threatened species in the world, called the Red List. Each species is labeled according to how at risk it is.

Least Concern: Not considered at risk.

Near Threatened: At risk of being vulnerable or endangered in the future.

Vulnerable: At risk of extinction.

Endangered: At high risk of extinction.

Critically Endangered: At extremely high risk of extinction.

Extinct in the Wild: Only lives in captivity.

Extinct: No members of a species are left.

China. They searched forests for bamboo. They found it on high slopes in summer. They found it in the valleys in winter. But China's population was growing. As more and more people lived in the country, they developed land where pandas had lived. Farmers plowed down the

bamboo to plant crops. The pandas had less food to eat. Hunters also killed many pandas. By the 1970s, approximately 1,000 pandas were left in the wild.

China set aside land for the pandas starting in the 1960s. It created strips of land known as bamboo trails. Giant pandas can follow them to the mountains. China also started a captive breeding program. Some baby pandas born in zoos are released into the wild as adults. The government has also cracked down on illegal hunting. An estimated 2,000 giant pandas live in the mountains of China, and another 200 live in zoos.

300
Weight in pounds (136 kg) of an adult giant panda.

Status: Endangered
Population: Approximately 2,000
Home: China
Life Span: 14–20 years

2

UTAH PRAIRIE DOGS GET BACK TO DIGGING

Prairie dogs belong to the squirrel family of rodents, but they get their name from their loud bark. They make this sound as a warning when they spot a danger. Prairie dogs live on grassy plains, in burrows they dig using their sharp claws. These underground homes have many rooms, with separate areas for sleeping, food storage, or waste. Prairie dogs once lived in communities of thousands or even millions.

When more people settled the western United States in the 1800s and 1900s, they did not want to live alongside prairie dogs. The prairie dogs' tunnels ruined land for crops, and the uneven ground over the burrows was dangerous for livestock. Prairie dogs also ate grasses

Utah prairie dogs eat grasses, flowers, seeds, and sometimes insects.

12

Length in inches
(30 cm) of an adult
prairie dog.

Status: Endangered
Population:
Approximately 9,200
adults
Home: Utah
Life Span: 3–4 years

A relative of
the squirrel,
prairie dogs only
live in North
America.

PRAIRIE DOG TOWNS

Prairie dogs live in big groups called towns. Usually a town covers less than half of one square mile (1.3 sq km). But one prairie dog town in Texas in the early 1900s filled 25,000 square miles (65,000 sq km). That's about the size of the state of West Virginia. Approximately 400 million prairie dogs used to live in this town before the land was developed.

that cows grazed on. Farmers and ranchers shot or poisoned thousands of prairie dogs in the early 1900s. The number of Utah prairie dogs fell from approximately 100,000 to approximately 3,500 by the 1970s.

Utah prairie dogs were added to the Endangered Species List in 1973. People thought this prairie dog would be extinct by 2000. Lands were set aside in places such as Bryce Canyon National Park. There prairie dog burrows would not be disturbed. Elsewhere, it was illegal to kill the prairie dogs. With these protections, they tripled in number.

BLACK-FOOTED FERRETS A SUCCESS STORY

Black-footed ferrets look like they are wearing masks. Their slim bodies let them slip into burrows made by other animals. There they search for their top prey, prairie dogs. But many prairie dog towns

Ferrets' slim bodies help them slide easily into the burrows of other animals.

1

Number of prairie dogs a ferret typically eats every three days.

Status: Endangered
Population:
   Approximately 1,000
Home: Western Great
   Plains
Life Span: 1–3 years

turned into ghost towns after people killed huge numbers of prairie dogs in the 1800s and 1900s. And the black-footed ferrets lost their main food source. Around 100 years ago, 500,000 black-footed ferrets lived in 12 states in the western Great Plains. But by the 1960s, they were thought to be extinct.

Then, in 1981, a pet dog in Wyoming brought home a dead black-footed ferret. Scientists searched the prairie until they found a colony of a few dozen ferrets. They were living in prairie dog burrows.

A few years later, the colony was struck by plague, and many died. Scientists stepped in to save the ferrets. They treated the burrows for fleas carrying the disease and took 18 healthy adult ferrets into captivity to breed. As their numbers increased, the ferrets were released to live in the wild.

Since then, their numbers have been climbing again. More than 7,000 ferrets have been released since 1991. As of 2011, approximately 1,000 black-footed ferrets once again were hunting prairie dogs in the wild.

FERRET BOOT CAMP

Ferrets that have been in captive breeding programs need training before they can be set free. So ferrets spend 30 days in "boot camp" learning skills to survive. They are trained to hunt prairie dogs in burrows. They also learn how to dodge predators, such as owls. Ferrets that finish "boot camp" are 10 times more likely to survive for several years in the wild.

FLORIDA PANTHERS SLOWLY ON THE RISE

Florida panthers once stalked prey across the southeastern United States. These big cats roamed forests and swamps. They hunted deer. They also killed cows and other livestock for food. People's desire to protect livestock meant that panthers became the hunted.

People killed so many panthers in the 1800s and early 1900s that they almost went extinct. They could only be found in the southern tip of Florida. But that soon became one of the fastest growing areas of the

AWARENESS HELPS

To help raise awareness about protecting panthers, the state started Save the Florida Panther Day. On this day, scientists educate people on how to live near panthers without harming them. Exhibits show people how to protect pets and livestock using special fences. They also remind drivers to be watchful on roadways where panthers might be crossing.

Panthers don't roar. They sometimes growl, purr, or hiss.

country. Panthers lost more habitat as houses were built. Cars on busy roads hit them. In 1989, land was set aside for a panther refuge, but it was almost too late. By the 1990s, scientists counted only 30 panthers in the wild. The group was so small that breeding occurred between panthers that were too closely related. This led to health problems, and many young panthers did not live long.

In 1995, scientists brought in eight female Texas cougars, a similar species. They started breeding with the panthers, and the population rose to more than 100 within a decade. Approximately 160 Florida panthers lived in the wild as of 2013. To help them survive, the

A Florida panther gets ready to hunt. Panthers usually eat deer.

state put up fences to keep them off highways and installed overpasses where they can cross roads safely.

7
Length in feet (2.1 m) of an adult Florida panther.

Status: Endangered
Population: Approximately 160
Home: Florida
Life Span: 12 years

THINK ABOUT IT

What else do you think residents of Florida could do to help the panthers? What kind of laws do you think might help to protect them?

5

HOWLS OF GRAY WOLVES HEARD AGAIN

The howls of gray wolves once could be heard all across North America. Wolves howl to communicate with each other. As the largest members of the canine family, they are related to dogs. Gray wolves travel and hunt in packs.

Wolves are predators. They hunt other animals for food. They eat elk, moose, and caribou. When US settlers started moving west in the 1800s, wolves expanded their diet to include livestock, such as cows. Ranchers started shooting

Gray wolves' coats are actually a mixture of white, brown, and black fur.

Individual gray wolves each have a unique howl.

the wolves to save their animals. Sometimes they left out poison bait or paid trappers to kill wolves. As wolf populations fell, cows could graze more safely. But gray wolves were gone from most states by the 1930s.

The Endangered Species Act started protecting gray wolves in 1973. Gray wolves from Canada were trapped and taken to Yellowstone National Park from 1994 through 1996. None had lived in the park since 1926, when the last wolf known to live in Yellowstone was shot. The wolf population started to climb again. Now the howls of 5,000 wolves can be heard in Yellowstone and other western regions. Another 7,000 or more wolves live in Alaska.

50
Square miles (129 sq km) a gray wolf's range typically covers.

Status: Least concern
US Population: 12,000
Home: Alaska, Idaho, Michigan, Minnesota, Montana, Wisconsin, and Wyoming
Life Span: 8–13 years

THINK ABOUT IT

Now that more wolves are thriving in the wild, what do you think ranchers should do to protect their livestock without harming the wolves?

RED WOLVES RETURN THANKS TO CAPTIVE BREEDING

Once a red wolf chooses a mate, the pair usually stays together for life. Red wolves hunt in packs consisting of a mated pair and their offspring. Each pack will mark its territory using its scent and defend it from other wolf packs. Red wolves once hunted all over the southeastern United States. They eat small mammals, such as raccoons and rodents, as well as insects and berries. By the 1900s, much of the red wolves' habitat had been turned into farmland. Ranchers trapped and shot them to keep them from hunting livestock. In 1980, the red wolf was extinct in the wild.

By then, the US Fish and Wildlife Service had rounded up 17 red wolves to start a breeding program. In 1987, enough red wolves had

Red wolves are smaller than their cousin, the gray wolf.

Red wolves make their dens in hollow trees or on stream banks.

been born to send some back into the wild. Four pairs were released on a refuge in North Carolina. Since the wolves were raised in captivity, scientists were relieved that they were able to hunt in the wild. By

2013, more than 100 wild-born wolves roamed free on 1.7 million acres (687,966 ha) of land. And 200 more red wolves live in US zoos.

Scientists have continued breeding programs on two islands. One is off the coast of South Carolina and the other is near Florida. Being on the islands helps red wolves to raise their pups in a setting that is more like their natural habitat. That way, when they are released in the wild in North Carolina, they have hunting and survival skills. Scientists try to pair the island wolves with mates in the wild to encourage breeding. This helps keep the species healthy.

20
Miles (32 km) per day a red wolf will travel looking for food.

Status: Critically endangered
Population: Approximately 130
Home: North Carolina
Life Span: 6–7 years

ISLAND FOXES MAKE SPEEDY RECOVERY

A subspecies of island foxes has lived on California's Catalina Island for approximately 4,000 years. The tiny foxes weigh approximately four to six pounds (1.8 to 2.7 kg)—about the size of a small cat. They eat mice, insects, lizards, berries, and fruit. The variety of their diet helps them to survive on the small island. But humans had to step in to save the foxes when sickness almost wiped them out.

Island foxes started becoming sick in 1998 with a form of distemper that usually affects raccoons. Another animal may have first brought the disease to the island. The foxes had never been exposed to the disease before and had no resistance. Their numbers fell from 1,300 to only 100 within a few years. They had been listed as threatened under the California Endangered Species Act

STRESS-FREE CHECKUPS

These foxes do not have natural predators on the island. So they are not on their guard like mainland foxes. That makes it easy for people to handle them. The foxes do not have to be drugged for exams. But people do put tiny masks on the foxes when it's time to draw blood to avoid being bitten.

since 1971 because of their small habitat. With this new threat, the foxes were considered endangered.

Medicine given to pets to prevent distemper did not work on the foxes. Scientists worked hard to come up

6

Number of island fox subspecies that live on islands off California's coast.

Status: Endangered
Population:
Approximately 1,500
Home: Catalina Island, California
Life Span: 4–6 years

foxes the shots and other medical treatment. They also put microchips under their skin for tracking. Free of sickness, the foxes started doing better. Now approximately 1,500 foxes roam the island. Most have had distemper shots. Pet owners also are encouraged to give their pets distemper shots to prevent the spread of the disease to wildlife.

with a new vaccination. When it was ready in 2004, they used cat food to trap foxes. Then they gave the

The island fox is the largest mammal on Catalina Island.

8

KEY DEER BOUNCE BACK ON BIG PINE KEY

Key deer only live on the Florida Keys. They are cousins to the white-tailed deer. Key deer are smaller in size because they adapted to the tiny islands where they live. They only weigh between 65 and 80 pounds (29–36 kg). Key deer live so close to people that they do not fear them. But this lack of fear can sometimes put the deer at risk.

Key deer are sometimes called toy deer because of their small size.

Drivers in the Florida Keys have to be on the lookout for Key deer that wander onto roads.

Settlers and sailors hunted Key deer in the early 1900s. Only 25 deer were left by the 1950s. That spurred the US Fish and Wildlife Service into action. It started the National Key Deer Refuge in 1957. This safe spot covers 25 islands in the Keys.

While they are no longer hunted, Key deer still face other dangers. Some people feed the deer even though it is against the law. This encourages the deer to beg for food. When they come into areas where people are, they are more likely to be hit by cars. The nighttime speed limit was lowered to help keep the deer safe. Fences also block the deer from wandering onto the main highway. Now 1,000 Key deer live on Big Pine Key.

160

Different kinds of plants eaten by Key deer.

Status: Least concern
Population: 1,000
Home: Florida Keys
Life Span: 3–6 years

THINK ABOUT IT

What could be done to prevent people from feeding Key deer? What words might you put on a road sign?

AMERICAN BISON ONCE AGAIN ROAM THE GREAT PLAINS

American bison can weigh more than one ton (900 kg). That's as much as a small car. They are the heaviest mammals in North America. This does not stop them from racing up to 40 miles per hour (64 km/h)

Bison live in herds, with females and calves staying close together for most of the year.

6.5

Height in feet (2 m) of an adult bison.

Status: Near threatened
Population:
Approximately 30,000 living in protected herds
Home: Great Plains
Life Span: 20–25 years

when they run! These giants of the Great Plains need to graze on huge amounts of grasses. But their days of roaming nearly ended.

Millions of bison once thundered across the plains. Then European settlers came. They shot approximately 50 million bison during the 1800s. Some shot them for sport. Others ate the meat. They turned the hides into robes. The huge herds shrank. Only 750 bison remained by the 1890s.

President Theodore Roosevelt wanted to bring back the bison. He and others helped found the American Bison Society. They sent bison to a preserve in the West. Approximately 30,000 bison total live in herds that are protected and monitored by the US government. A wild herd of approximately 4,000 roams Yellowstone National Park. Another 200,000 bison live on private ranches where they are raised for meat.

DEADLY SPECIALS

Railroads stretched across the Great Plains in the 1870s. People viewed bison as pests. Herds delayed trains. They ruined miles of track. Railroads offered hunting "specials." People could shoot at bison from the trains. Rotting bison piled up on either side of the tracks. The smell made people sick. So many bison were killed that railroads stopped the specials.

SOUTHERN WHITE RHINOS SAVED FROM EXTINCTION

Southern white rhinoceroses are actually gray, not white. Their tough-looking skin is very sensitive to bug bites and sunburn. Rhinos roll in the mud because it is soothing. These animals are one of the biggest on Earth. They can weigh up to 6,000 pounds (2,272 kg). Their huge heads make up 2,000 pounds (907 kg) of that weight. They graze about half the time that they are awake. But their size made rhinos easy targets.

These rhinos once ranged across southern Africa. By 1892, they were believed to be extinct. Hunters

Male rhinos use their horns to fight off attackers.

White rhinos use water and mud to soothe their skin.

had shot most of the white rhinos. People in Asia prized the horns and paid a lot of money for them. They ground them up to make medicine. But there is no proof that rhino horn cures any illness.

Yet the rhino had survived. In 1895, a group of approximately 100 rhinos turned up in South Africa. People started breeding them on ranches. Some of the rhinos were then relocated to protected areas. By 2013, their numbers had increased to 20,000. They are no longer considered endangered, but African

countries where they live continue to have laws against hunting them.

120
Pounds (54 kg) of grass a southern white rhino eats in a day.

Status: Near threatened
Population:
 Approximately 20,000
Home: South Africa, Namibia, Zimbabwe, and Kenya
Life Span: 40 years

GRIZZLY BEARS BENEFIT FROM PROTECTION

Grizzly bears are huge, powerful animals. They stand up to eight feet (2.4 m) tall and can weigh as much as 800 pounds (363 kg). These giants eat mostly roots, fruits, and nuts, and sometimes small animals and fish. In the winter, they hibernate in caves or hillside dens. But as people developed the land where they lived, grizzly bears' options for food and shelter became limited.

As many as 50,000 grizzly bears may have roamed the United States several hundred years ago. But as people cut down forests for cities and farmland, the bears' natural food sources shrank. When bears wandered onto ranchland looking for food, they were shot. The US population

Grizzly bears also are known as brown bears.

Grizzly bear cubs separate from their mothers when they are approximately two years old.

dropped down to just 140 by the 1970s. Most of the remaining grizzly bears lived in the protected area of Yellowstone National Park.

In 1975, the Endangered Species Act made it illegal to kill grizzly bears. Since then, their population in the Rocky Mountains has grown to between 600 and 800. Another 600 live in Yellowstone. More land outside of Yellowstone has been set aside for the bears so that their numbers can continue to grow.

30
Miles per hour (48 km/h) that a grizzly bear can run.

Status: Least concern
Population: 1,200–1,400
Home: Yellowstone National Park, Rocky Mountains
Life Span: 25 years

LIVING NEAR BEARS

People used to kill grizzly bears that came looking for food in campgrounds, ranches, or cities. Since that became illegal, humans and bears have found ways to co-exist. Many campgrounds now use bear-proof trash bins. Beekeepers protect beehives with fences so bears can't get in.

12

SIBERIAN TIGERS ON THE PROWL THROUGH RUSSIA'S FORESTS

Siberian tigers have bold stripes. No two tigers have the same pattern. Their thick fur keeps them warm in the cold forests of Russia. These tigers are the largest wild cats on Earth. Hunting laws saved these fierce cats from extinction.

Siberian tigers roam far to find prey. They hide until they spot elk.

Siberian tigers have thick coats of fur to protect them in the cold.

Siberian tigers live alone except during mating season.

30 Siberian tigers were living in the wild by the 1940s.

The Soviet Union banned the hunting of tigers in 1947. Luckily the tigers had room to roam in Russia. Few people lived in their forest habitat. And not many trees were cut down. As they were hunted less, the tigers' numbers rose. An estimated 400 to 500 Siberian tigers lived in the forests of Russia by 2013.

Then they pounce. But hunters also laid in wait for tigers. People shot them. They turned tigers' fur into rugs and sold their claws as good luck charms. They mounted tiger heads as trophies, and they turned body parts into medicine. Only 20 to

18
Age in months when a Siberian tiger learns to hunt.

Status: Endangered
Population: 400–500
Home: Russia
Life Span: 14 years

FACT SHEET

- Many countries have laws protecting endangered animals. In 1973, the US Congress passed the Endangered Species Act. It requires state and federal government agencies to monitor and protect species that might become extinct. It also bans people from hunting, catching, trading, or possessing animals and plants that are protected.

- Many countries have laws against hunting certain wild animals that are protected, but these laws can be difficult to enforce. People who break these laws are called poachers. They continue to kill rare animals such as rhinos, elephants, and giant pandas to sell the valuable horns, tusks, or furs.

- The two US federal agencies that deal with endangered species are the US Fish and Wildlife Service and the National Oceanic and Atmospheric Administration. Both have departments dedicated to identifying and helping endangered species.

- Animals live in ecosystems, which are communities of living things that are connected to each other. When one species in an ecosystem does not do well, other species are affected, too. In prairie areas, for example, animals such as ferrets and coyotes depend on prairie dogs for food. In Yellowstone Park, gray wolves cause herds of elk to travel around. The elk spread seeds for aspen and willow trees. This helps the park's ecosystem become balanced, and animals such as beavers return.

- Sometimes when one species does well, it helps another come back. Red wolves are helping some North Carolina birds rebound. Birds such as quail and turkey lay their eggs in nests on the ground. Raccoons raided these nests. But now that wolves are around, they prey on the raccoons. More eggs can hatch.

- Giant pandas in the wild stay away from people, so scientists can only study their behavior in zoos. Thirteen American zoos have had panda residents. All zoo pandas are leased from the Chinese government, and cubs born in zoos are returned to China.

- While several mammals have made comebacks, many more species are still on the endangered list. The IUCN lists two mammals that are extinct in the wild: Pere David's deer and scimitar-horned oryx, a kind of antelope. Another 196 mammals are considered critically endangered, and 447 are endangered.

GLOSSARY

burrow
A hole or tunnel dug as a living space.

captive breeding
Saving a species by breeding them in environments controlled by humans.

distemper
A disease caused by a virus that affects animals.

endangered
Threatened with extinction.

extinct
The death of all members of a species.

habitat
The place where a plant or animal naturally lives or grows.

key
A small low-lying coral island.

pack
A group of animals that live and hunt together.

plague
The outbreak of a disease that spreads rapidly and kills great numbers.

poacher
Someone who hunts or fishes illegally.

predator
An animal that kills or eats another animal.

prey
An animal that is hunted or killed by another animal for food.

species
A group of animals or plants that are similar and can produce young.

threatened
In danger of becoming extinct.

FOR MORE INFORMATION

Books

Boothroyd, Jennifer. *Endangered and Extinct Mammals*. Minneapolis: Lerner Publishing Group, 2014.

Marsh, Laura. *National Geographic Readers: Tigers*. Washington, DC: National Geographic Children's Books, 2012.

Portman, Michael. *Pandas in Danger*. New York: Gareth Stevens Publishing, 2012.

Taylor, Barbara. *The Mammal Book: Jaws, Paws, Claws and More*. New York: Carlton Books, 2010.

Websites

Discovery Education: Animals of North America
www.discoveryeducation.com/northamerica

National Geographic Kids: Animals and Pets
kids.nationalgeographic.com/kids/animals

US Fish and Wildlife Service: Endangered Species for Kids
www.fws.gov/endangered/education

INDEX

About the Author

Nancy Furstinger is the author of almost 100 books, including many on animals. She has been a feature writer for a daily newspaper, a managing editor of trade and consumer magazines, and an editor at two children's book publishing houses.

READ MORE FROM 12-STORY LIBRARY

Every 12-Story Library book is available in many formats, including Amazon Kindle and Apple iBooks. For more information, visit your device's store or 12StoryLibrary.com.